SCENE BY SCENE
COMPARATIVE WORKBOOK HL17

A Doll's House

by Henrik Ibsen

Theme/Issue - Relationships

Literary Genre

General Vision and Viewpoint

Copyright © 2016 by Amy Farrell.

All rights reserved. No part of this publication may be reproduced, distributed or transmitted in any form or by any means, including photocopying, recording, or other electronic or mechanical methods, without the prior written permission of the publisher, except in the case of brief quotations embodied in critical reviews and certain other noncommercial uses permitted by copyright law. For permission requests, write to the publisher, addressed "Attention: Permissions Coordinator," at the address below.

Scene by Scene
11 Millfield, Enniskerry
Wicklow, Ireland.
www.scenebysceneguides.com

info@scenebysceneguides.com

A Doll's House Comparative Workbook HL17 by Amy Farrell. —1st ed.
ISBN 978-1-910949-43-6

A Doll's House Comparative Study Workbook

This workbook is designed to help Leaving Certificate English students become familiar with the Comparative Study modes and to understand how each mode may be applied to *A Doll's House*.

The Comparative Study Modes at Higher Level for 2017 are:

Theme/Issue

The theme covered in this workbook is Relationships. This theme can be applied to any relationship in a text and covers love, marriage, friendship and family bonds.

Consider the complexities of relationships and the impact they have on characters' lives.

Literary Genre

This mode refers to the way the story is told.

Consider aspects of narration such as the manner and style of narration, characterisation, setting, tension, literary techniques, etc.

The General Vision and Viewpoint

This mode refers to the author's outlook or view of life and how this viewpoint is represented in the text.

Consider whether the text is bright or dark, optimistic or pessimistic, uplifting or bleak, etc.

How Does it Work?

This workbook has three parts, one each for Theme/Issue (our chosen theme for study is Relationships), Literary Genre and General Vision and Viewpoint. Each part has three sections: Know the Text, Know the Mode and Compare the Texts.

Know The Text

These questions are on the *A Doll's House* text and refer specifically to this play. Through answering these questions you will get to know the text well, while also getting a feel for the Comparative Study mode the questions relate to.

Know the Mode

These questions use 'mode' specific terms and phrases and are intended to help prepare you for tackling exam questions. They focus on the mode itself, rather than the text you have studied. You apply your knowledge of the text to the mode in question.

Compare the Texts

These questions ask you to compare your texts under specific aspects of each mode. It is important that you get used to the idea of comparing and contrasting your chosen texts, as this is what the Comparative Study is all about. It is good practice to think about your texts in terms of their similarities and differences within each mode.

This approach is designed to prevent 'drift' between modes and focuses on analysis and personal response, rather than summary.

KNOW THE TEXT

Theme/Issue - Know the Text

1 What are your first impressions of Nora and Torvald's marriage?

2 How does Nora behave around her husband? Why does she behave this way?

3 Torvald does not allow Nora to eat macaroons. What is your response to this? What does it suggest about their relationship?

4 How did Nora save her husband's life? Why does she have to keep this a secret?

KNOW THE TEXT

5 Is Nora a dutiful, obedient wife in the first two Acts?

6 Is Torvald a controlling husband?

A DOLL'S HOUSE – THEME/ISSUE – RELATIONSHIPS

7 Does Torvald treat Nora like a child?
Does Nora act like a child around him?

8 How does Torvald view his wife?

KNOW THE TEXT

9 Is their relationship important to Nora and Torvald? Explain.

10 Does Torvald care about and understand his wife? Give examples to support your view.

11 Does Nora care about and understand her husband? Give examples to support your view.

12 Does Torvald have a realistic view of their marriage?

KNOW THE TEXT

13 Does Torvald really know his wife?
Does Nora really know him?

14 Are there elements of pretence and fantasy in their relationship?

A DOLL'S HOUSE - THEME/ISSUE - RELATIONSHIPS

15 Are Torvald and Nora a good match?
Does their relationship bring them happiness?

16 Is this a positive or negative relationship?

17 What **strengths** do you see in Nora and Torvald's marriage?

18 What **weaknesses** or problems do you see in Nora and Torvald's marriage?

A DOLL'S HOUSE - THEME/ISSUE - RELATIONSHIPS

19 How does their relationship **change** and **develop**?

20 How does the title of the play relate to Nora and Torvald's relationship?

KNOW THE TEXT

21 What sort of relationship did Nora have with her father?

22 Does Dr. Rank have a good, meaningful relationship with the Helmers?

23 Do Mrs Linde and Krogstad have a good relationship? Is it better or worse than that of Nora and Torvald?

24 Does Nora do the right thing, when she walks out on her husband?

Theme/Issue - Know the Mode

25 Are relationships in this text generally **positive** (warm, supportive, nurturing, genuine) or **negative** (cold, cruel, destructive, false)?

26. What makes relationships in this text complicated and **difficult**?

27 What would **improve** relationships in this text?

A DOLL'S HOUSE - THEME/ISSUE - RELATIONSHIPS

28 How do relationships **change** during the story?

KNOW THE MODE

29 What did **you learn** about relationships from viewing this play?

30 Are relationships **portrayed realistically** in this text? Make use of examples to support the points you make.

KNOW THE MODE

31 Are relationships in this story **interesting** and **involving**?

A DOLL'S HOUSE - THEME/ISSUE - RELATIONSHIPS

32 Did anything about the theme of relationships in this text **shock**, **upset** or **unsettle** you?

33

What is the **most signficant relationship** in this text?
What makes it so significant and important?

34 Do relationships in this story bring characters **happiness** or **sorrow**?

35 Choose **key moments** from this story that highlight relationships in the text.

COMPARE THE TEXTS

Theme/Issue - Compare the Texts

36 Were relationships in *A Doll's House* more positive and supportive than the relationships in your other texts? Give specific examples.

37 Rank the relationships you have studied in your various texts from most positive to most negative. Add a note to explain your choices.

38 Were relationships in *A Doll's House* the most engaging and interesting that you have studied? Explain your choice.

A DOLL'S HOUSE - THEME/ISSUE - RELATIONSHIPS

39 Rank the relationships you have studied in your various texts from most interesting to least interesting. Add a note to explain your choices.

40 Did you **learn most** about the theme of relationships from this text or another text on your comparative course?

41 What **similarities** do you notice in the theme of relationships in this text and your other comparative texts?

A DOLL'S HOUSE - THEME/ISSUE - RELATIONSHIPS

42 What **differences** do you notice in the theme of relationships in this text and your other comparative texts?

COMPARE THE TEXTS

Literary Genre - Know the Text

43 How is this story told? (Consider the play format).

44 Why is the story told in this way?
What is the effect of this?

KNOW THE TEXT

45 What is your initial view of Nora?

46 How does Ibsen develop Nora's character?

A DOLL'S HOUSE – LITERARY GENRE

47 Which version of Nora do you prefer? Explain your choice.

48 How does Ibsen show us Torvald's selfish, childish side? Is there more to him then this? Explain your view.

KNOW THE TEXT

49 What role does Mrs Linde play in the story?

50 Did you expect Mrs Linde to stop Krogstad from telling Torvald everything?
Was this development unexpected?

A DOLL'S HOUSE – LITERARY GENRE

51 What role does Krogstad play in the story?

52 How does Krogstad's letter create **tension** and **suspense**?

KNOW THE TEXT

53 What does reading Krogstad's letter reveal about Torvald? Does Nora's reaction surprise you?

54 Is Krogstad a typical villian? Explain your point of view.

| 55 | What role does Dr. Rank play in the story? |

| 56 | How does Dr Rank's illness contribute to the story? |

57 Is Nora leaving an **unexpected twist**?

58 Is this a play about duty and identity or something else?

59 *A Doll's House* was considered to be very controversial when it was first performed. Why was this, do you think?
Is it still controversial today?

Literary Genre - Know the Mode

60 Did **you** enjoy the **storyline** of the text?
Was it exciting/compelling/tense/emotional?
Why/why not?

61 Is there just one **plot** or many plots?
What connections can you make between the storylines?

62 What three things interested **you** most in the story?

KNOW THE MODE

63 Are **characters** vivid, realistic and well-developed?

64 Do **you** empathise or **identify** with any character(s)?
Did you become involved in this story or care about the characters? Use examples.

65 Who was your **favourite character**?
What aspects of this character did you enjoy?

KNOW THE MODE

66 Consider Nora as the play's **heroine**. What made Nora a **memorable** or **interesting** character?

67 Who was your **least favourite character**? What aspects of this character did you dislike? What made them a memorable or interesting character?

KNOW THE MODE

68 Is the story humorous or tragic, romantic or realistic? Explain using examples.

69 To what **genre** does it belong?
What aspects of this genre did **you** enjoy?
Is it Romance, Thriller, Horror, Action/Adventure, Historical, Fantasy, Science-fiction, Satire, etc.?

70 How does the playwright create **suspense**, **high emotion** and **excitement** in the text? What **techniques** does he use to good advantage?

KNOW THE MODE

71 Consider the playwright's use of **tension** and **resolution** in the play. What are the major **tensions/problems/conflicts** in the text? Are they **resolved** or not?

A DOLL'S HOUSE – LITERARY GENRE

72 Did the playwright make use of any striking patterns of **imagery** or **symbols** to add to the story?

73 How does the playwright make use of the **unexpected** in this text? What did this add to the story? (Think about key moments here.)

KNOW THE MODE

74 What is the **climax** (high point) of the story?

75 What did **you** think of this moment?
How did it make **you feel**?

A DOLL'S HOUSE - LITERARY GENRE

76 Comment on the **language** of the play.
How does this spoken dimension add to the story?

77 Comment on the **pacing** of the play.
How does this add to the story?

78 Comment on the **setting** of the play. *Consider time, place, and the sole location of the Helmers' home. How does setting add to your understanding of the characters and their story?*

79 Was anything about this play **moving** or **emotional**?
Think of moments in the play that you responded to. What made them moving? How did this add to the story?

80 On a scale of one to ten, how much did you enjoy the **ending**? What was satisfying/unsatisfying about it? Was anything left unanswered?

A DOLL'S HOUSE – LITERARY GENRE

81 The experiences of seeing a play, reading a novel and viewing a film are very different.
What aspects of the **play form** worked well in this story, in your opinion?

82 What did **you** like about **the way** the story was told?
*Mention aspects of storytelling and literary techniques that **you** found enjoyable. Refer to key moments.*

83 Identify **key moments** in the play that illustrate Literary Genre (the way the story is told). Clearly **define literary techniques/aspects of narrative** in your analysis.

Literary Genre - Compare the Texts

84 Did **you** like the way this story was told more than your other comparative texts?
State what you enjoyed most about each.

85 Is *A Doll's House* more **exciting** than your other texts?
Consider tension, pacing, suspense, conflict and the unexpected.

86 Are **characters** more engaging in this play than in your other texts?
Refer to each of your texts in you answer.

87 Is the **setting** more effective in telling this story than in your other texts?
Refer to each of your texts in your answer.

88 Is this story more **unpredictable** than your other texts?
Refer to each of your texts in your answer.

COMPARE THE TEXTS

89 Did this play have greater **emotional power** than your other texts?
Was emotional power created in a more interesting way here or in a different text?

90 What **similarities** do you notice in the Literary Genre of this play and your other comparative texts?
Mention specific aspects of narrative.

COMPARE THE TEXTS

91 What **differences** do you notice in the Literary Genre of this play and your other comparative texts?
Mention specific aspects of narrative.

COMPARE THE TEXTS

A DOLL'S HOUSE - GENERAL VISION AND VIEWPOINT

General Vision and Viewpoint - Know the Text

92 Do Nora and Torvald love and support one another? Is their marriage a positive or negative comment on life?

93 Is Nora under a lot of pressure in this play? Rank the three things that put her under the most pressure or stress.
What does her need for secrecy reveal about her situation? Is this positive or negative?

94 How do **you** feel about the fact that she had to conceal so much from her husband?

95 What reaction did Nora wish for from Torvald when he learned what she had done? Did she get the reaction she hoped for?

A DOLL'S HOUSE – GENERAL VISION AND VIEWPOINT

96 Were you disappointed by Torvald's reaction? Explain your view.

97 What does Torvald's reaction to Nora's 'crime' reveal about the playwright's outlook?

KNOW THE TEXT

98 What was your reaction to Krogstad's threats? What motivated him to act as he did? Is this a positive or negative comment on human nature?

99 Does Ibsen offer a positive or negative view of love and marriage?

100 Does the rekindling of Krogstad and Mrs Linde's relationship offer a positive or negative comment on life? Explain your view.

101 Did you anticipate a **happy ending**?
Is there a happy ending?
Explain your answer.

102 Is Nora's future promising as the play ends? Explain your view.

103 Is Torvald's future promising as the play ends? Explain your view.

A DOLL'S HOUSE – GENERAL VISION AND VIEWPOINT

104 Is the future promising for other characters as the play ends?

105 How does Nora walking out on her family affect the General Vision and Viewpoint of the play?

KNOW THE TEXT

106 Is Nora being decisive and independent or cruel and selfish as the play ends?

107 What is Henrik Ibsen telling us about life in this story?
What is Henrik Ibsen's message?
Is his outlook positive or negative, in your view?

General Vision and Viewpoint - Know the Mode

108 Identify bright/hopeful/optimistic aspects of the play.

KNOW THE MODE

109 Identify dark/hopeless/pessimistic aspects of the play.

110 Is this text **optimistic** or **pessimistic**? Explain. *Consider characters' happiness, imagery, atmosphere, future prospects, etc.*

111 On a scale of one to ten, how optimistic is this text?

KNOW THE MODE

112 Identify the **aspects of life** that the playwright concentrates on.
Are they positive or negative?
Consider secrecy, identity, bravery, duty, loyalty, etc.

A DOLL'S HOUSE - GENERAL VISION AND VIEWPOINT

113 What **comments** do characters make on their **society** and the problems they're facing?

KNOW THE MODE

114 Are characters happy or unhappy?

115 What makes characters in this story happy and fulfilled?

A DOLL'S HOUSE - GENERAL VISION AND VIEWPOINT

116 What makes characters in this story unhappy and unfulfilled?

117 Are **relationships** destructive or nurturing? What do they reveal about life, as we see characters supported/thwarted in their efforts to grow/mature?

118 Are **imagery** and **language** bright or dark in the text? (Tone of the text)

119 What is the **mood** of this text?

KNOW THE MODE

120 What does this story **teach us about life**?
What do we learn about life's hardships? Are struggles overcome? Is determination rewarded? Is life difficult or joyful?

121 How do you **feel** as you watch this play?
Refer to key moments to anchor your answer.

KNOW THE MODE

122 How do you **feel** at the **end**?

123 Are **questions** raised by the text **resolved** by the end?
Are they resolved **happily** or **unhappily**?

124 Are **you hopeful** or **despairing** regarding the prospects for human **happiness** in this story?
Are characters likely to be happy?

A DOLL'S HOUSE – GENERAL VISION AND VIEWPOINT

125 Identify the **key moments** in the play that illustrate the General Vision and Viewpoint of the text.

General Vision and Viewpoint - Compare the Texts

126 Is life happier for characters in this story than in your other comparative texts? Explain.

127 Do characters in this text face more obstacles and difficulties than in your other texts?
Who struggles most?

128 Are characters in this text **rewarded more** for their struggles than in your other texts?
By overcoming adversity, do they achieve true happiness and contentment in a way that is not realised in your other texts?

129 Is this the brightest, most hopeful and triumphant text you have studied? Explain why its message is more or less positive than your other texts.

130 Which of your chosen texts was the bleakest and most upsetting or depressing?
Explain why it was more negative than your other texts. What made them more positive?

COMPARE THE TEXTS

131 Plot your three texts on a scale of one to ten, from darkest (most pessimistic) to brightest (most optimistic). Add points to explain their position.

132 What **similarities** do you notice in the General Vision and Viewpoint of this text and your other comparative texts?

COMPARE THE TEXTS

A DOLL'S HOUSE – GENERAL VISION AND VIEWPOINT

133 What **differences** do you notice in the General Vision and Viewpoint of this text and your other comparative texts?

COMPARE THE TEXTS

www.ingramcontent.com/pod-product-compliance
Lightning Source LLC
Chambersburg PA
CBHW050714090526
44587CB00019B/3370